Doing Business in
China

JIHONG SANDERSON

London, New York, Melbourne,
Munich, and Delhi

Senior Editor Peter Jones
Senior Art Editor Helen Spencer
Executive Managing Editor Adèle Hayward
Managing Art Editor Kat Mead
Art Director Peter Luff
Publisher Stephanie Jackson
Production Editor Ben Marcus
Production Controller Hema Gohil
US Editor Charles Wills

Produced for Dorling Kindersley Limited by

cobaltid

The Stables, Wood Farm, Deopham Road,
Attleborough, Norfolk NR17 1AJ
www.cobaltid.co.uk

Editors Louise Abbott, Kati Dye, Maddy King,
Marek Walisiewicz
Designers Darren Bland, Claire Dale, Paul Reid,
Annika Skoog, Lloyd Tilbury, Shane Whiting

First American Edition, 2008

Published in the United States by DK Publishing
375 Hudson Street, New York, New York 10014

08 09 10 11   10 9 8 7 6 5 4 3 2 1

DD473—September 2008

Published in Great Britain by
Dorling Kindersley Limited.

A catalog record for this book is available from
the Library of Congress.

ISBN 978-0-7566-3707-1

DK books are available at special discounts
when purchased in bulk for sales promotions,
premiums, fund-raising, or educational use.
For details, contact: DK Publishing Special Markets,
375 Hudson Street, New York, New York 10014 or
SpecialSales@dk.com.

Color reproduction
by Colourscan, Singapore
Printed in China by WKT

Discover more at **www.dk.com**

Contents

Introduction

China—one of the world's largest and fastest-growing markets—has been called "the business opportunity of this generation." But business in China is unlike business in any other country—China is different. Understanding how Chinese history, culture, and business practices affect China-related ventures is essential if you are to maximize the opportunities and avoid unpleasant and costly pitfalls.

This concise book provides you with the comprehensive yet practical information required as a foundation for your success in China. It provides the inside knowledge of Chinese business culture that you need to find and take advantage of the opportunities in China-related enterprise: how to entertain Chinese clients, how to negotiate a workable Chinese contract, and how to effectively manage Chinese colleagues, suppliers, and employees.

Doing Business in China tells you all you need to know about how to get things done in China, from navigating local bureaucracy to risk management. When a reporter asked Larry Ellison, CEO of Oracle Corporation, what was the biggest risk of doing business in China, he answered, "The biggest risk is not investing in China. That is a mistake we are not going to make." For those firms prepared to approach this market with care and understanding, the potential rewards are huge.

Chapter 1

Business profile

What is China like today, and why is it unique? Large-scale development and market growth is apparent almost everywhere, and foreign companies have an unprecedented opportunity to share in that growth. However, the history, politics, economy, and current trends of this vast country explain why business there requires a different approach.

Many Chinas, rapid change

With its mutually unintelligible dialects, powerful local governments—with their border checkpoints between some cities and provinces—China can seem more like a loose alliance of states than one country. But all of the different Chinas share one characteristic: large-scale, very rapid change.

Changing goals

China is part way through a transition of goals, from idealistic to practical. In 1949 Mao Zedong united the Chinese people with a vision of a utopian society without poverty, hunger, violence, or inequality. In 1978, however, China's then leader, Deng Xiaopeng, redirected China on a search for practical solutions to national problems: "It doesn't matter if the cat is black or white, as long as it catches the mouse." China's goals today are a mix of the idealistic and the practical, so Western business contacts need to understand and be sensitive to both aspects.

Demographic change

China is constantly reinventing itself. The "current model" of this evolving society seeks prosperity, an excellent education for the one child in each family, an environment with clean water, air, and soil, and better lives for its poorest citizens. Meanwhile, China's new middle class of business people, scientists, teachers, and technicians is now estimated to number about 250 million people, all seeking consumables—from property, cars, and vacations, to financial services.

The new market economy

Business survival in China in the past depended on official policy, rather than market considerations; managed centrally from Beijing, each business adopted the products, output level, and pricing, as well as the suppliers and customers, that government planners specified. Customer satisfaction, market share, and profitability have only begun to exert an influence in the past generation and, as with China's legal system, the market economy is still a work in progress. Harmonizing with government policy and recruiting powerful sponsors for business projects is still vital to success.

TIP

BE PREPARED
Those who visited China before 2000 are likely to be most impressed by the transformation in its urban landscapes and infrastructure. However, never decline invitations to visit and admire scenic and historic sites—even if you have seen them before—as these remain an ongoing source of intense national pride.

IN FOCUS... RULE BY LAW

Like the cities of China, Chinese law is mostly new. In 1949, China abolished its existing laws, replacing them with a set of general principles applied by the political leadership. Almost all of the approximately 2,500 lawyers and judges practicing after 1949 were sent to re-education labor camps during the Cultural Revolution (1966–76).

By the late 1970s when China began to open up, there was little or no legal system. The period since 1978 has seen a rapid transition from rule by powerful individuals toward rule by law. The task is not yet complete, but today China has over 118,000 lawyers presenting 5 million cases annually before more than 190,000 judges.

Country profile

China is a land and people on a massive scale. It has a land area similar to that of the US, yet more than four times the population. It is estimated that there are more people studying English in China than there are native English-speakers in the world.

Capital/largest city: **Beijing/Shanghai**

Population: **1.321 billion (2007)**

Official languages: **1 written (Mandarin), 10 major spoken languages**

GDP/GDP per capita: **US$3.43 trillion (2007)/US$2,594 (based on exchange rate) or US$7,800 PPP***

Currency: **l yuan (¥) or renminbi (RMB) = 10 jiao = 100 fen**

Time zone: **All of mainland China observes Beijing Time: UTC +8**

Dialing code: **+86**

Principal business areas: **Shenzhen/Hong Kong, Shanghai, Beijing**

*PPP—*Purchasing Power Parity; many common goods and services can cost 50 percent to 75 percent less in China, compared with Europe or the US, after converting into local currency. This complicates calculations for both GDP and wages.*

The Chinese miracle

China's population includes 700 million people in rural areas who mostly struggle to make a living from small plots of land, as well as 400 million who travel via expressways, subways, and wide boulevards to their work in ultra-modern offices, shopping malls, and factories. With a literacy rate exceeding 90 percent and an excellent work ethic, the latter produce much of the world's clothing, toys, and household and electronic goods. China's GDP has had a growth rate averaging 10 percent annually for the last 25 years, and this astonishing economic growth has resulted in what is termed the "Chinese miracle"—the lifting out of desperate poverty of more than 100 million people.

Why do business in China?

Since China first opened its doors to global business in 1978, its economy has grown from ¥*362 billion to a staggering ¥24,662 billion. This means that China needs more of everything—much more—from iron ore to investment banking services. Experts say that China's position in global business is unprecedented in world history. Its astounding economic growth and sheer scale make it one of the top opportunities of this era.

The yuan (¥) or renminbi (RMB) — different names for the Chinese monetary unit, which is tied to a "basket" of global currencies. The exchange rate varied from 1.49 to the US dollar in 1980, to 8.35 in 1995, and 7.00 in 2008.

Savings and investment

Recent figures have placed China's national savings rate at around 40 percent of income—compared with slightly below zero for the US. This trend, plus China's economic growth, means that Chinese individuals and companies are likely to play an increasing role as global investors. Chinese acquisitions of foreign companies, their massive purchases of foreign government bonds, and their investments in foreign natural resources all underline China's growing financial resources. In addition to domestic capital accumulation, China continues to rank number one among the world's preferred destinations for foreign direct investment. This huge accumulation of wealth is the main underlying engine driving today's countless opportunities in China.

CULTURAL ANTENNAE

A bias toward action

Modern China is very entrepreneurial. In many parts of the world, building a refinery, chemical plant, or major manufacturing facility is a real challenge. Hesitant investors, uncertain local citizens, antagonistic special interest groups, and excessively zealous lawyers can delay or prevent even the most necessary and profitable projects in some countries. But in China, with hospitable local leaders, well funded policy banks (banks that base lending decisions largely on national goals, not profit), and over 270 welcoming industrial parks, good projects often receive "fast track" attention.

IN FOCUS...
THE CHINESE WORKFORCE

China's population of 1.3 billion includes 350 million agricultural workers with an average annual income of US$460, providing an almost endless reservoir of very low-cost labor. Urban workers, earning an average of US$1,475 per year, include almost 200 million experienced industrial workers and over 240 million experienced service employees. Highly educated workers also draw business to China. Taking advantage of a low-cost, high-talent labor pool, more than 750 foreign firms have established research facilities in China. Chinese universities produce about five million new graduates and over 8,000 science and engineering doctoral degree-holders per year. Even so, there is a growing shortage of skilled workers and managers.

China's market size

About 250 million people belong to China's rapidly growing middle class, able to afford a range of goods and services, from televisions and refrigerators, to medical care and advanced education for their children. As a result, China is now reportedly the largest market for mobile phones, internet use, TVs, and ATM machines, and will soon become the world's biggest consumer of meat, coal, grain, steel, fruit and vegetables, gold, decorative stone and wood products, solar energy and wind power equipment, semiconductors, and IPOs (initial public offerings on the stock market). Financial services are growing explosively from a very small base, with consumer debt increasing annually at 50 percent, home mortgages at 58 percent, student loans at 170 percent, and insurance assets at 54 percent.

China also has a vibrant and rapidly growing wealthy class. China is home to 66 billionaires and 345,000 millionaires (in US dollars), helping to make it the world's third-largest market for luxury goods. A generation ago affluent Chinese moved abroad to achieve a luxurious lifestyle. Now the mansions, country clubs, and most desirable brands are available in China. Bentley, Buick, BMW, and Audi all sell more cars in China than in their home markets—and usually at higher margins.

Chinese history and business

Before 1840, China's economy, government, philosophy, arts, and innovations were the envy of the world. China has never forgotten its glorious past and the reversals, at the hands of the Western powers and Japan, that ended its dominance. Understanding and being sensitive to this pattern of history strongly influences your success in modern China.

TIP

DO YOUR HOMEWORK
Many of the innovations that powered the industrial and military development of the West were based on Chinese inventions. Demonstrating your knowledge in this area can be a valuable business and social aid.

China past and present

Many Chinese consider China's current economic growth as a return to their correct and normal position in the world, not as a new development. For 2,000 years before 1840, the Chinese economy was either the largest or second largest in the world. The modern Chinese take great pride in this history. But there followed a century rife with painful issues for the Chinese: subjugation to Western powers following the Opium Wars (1839–42 and 1856–60); the Japanese invasion; and China's own civil war. After independence in 1949, Mao and his close followers were—and still are—regarded as national heroes for restoring peace and independence. For the Chinese, their contribution greatly outweighs the social problems associated with the Great Leap Forward and Cultural Revolution, and are not issues that foreign business people can debate.

CULTURAL ANTENNAE

Foreign relationships

Based on China's history, the Chinese often exhibit a "love–hate" relationship with foreigners that can enhance or endanger your Asian business ventures. On one hand, people in China admire Western technology, education, wealth, and power. Many advertisements and fashion displays portray models with European features, and many families dream of sending their children to Western universities. On the other hand, China's treatment at the hands of foreign governments, suffering humiliating occupations and devastating wars, still influences current attitudes.

Ancient China's innovations

Ancient Chinese rulers implemented civil service examinations, an efficient national postal system, and water and land expressways to transport goods and people over long distances.

One thousand years before the pyramids were built in Egypt, Chinese craftspeople were creating beautiful religious and artistic artifacts from bronze, pottery, and semiprecious stone.

More than 1,500 years before Gutenberg "invented" the printing press, Chinese printers used movable type to reproduce books on religion and philosophy.

The Chinese established a recipe for gunpowder, used to make fireworks and explosive weapons, in 1044 – 200 years before it appeared in Europe.

China's banknotes pre-date the first European use of paper money by 600 years, and as a consequence the Chinese also invented currency inflation and counterfeiting.

The flow of goods from China, paid for in precious metals, so depleted Europe's gold and silver reserves that in 65 BCE the Roman Senate tried to limit the wearing of silk.

Possibly the first recorded case of industrial espionage involved smuggling out of China the technology behind silk production.

China's evolving position in global business

In recent history, Chinese business has faced three simultaneous transitions: from undeveloped, centrally managed, and isolated, to developed, market-directed, and fully integrated into the world economy. As each of its industries reaches a new stage in the process, strategies for success change.

Creating markets

In 1978, the establishment of free markets for agricultural production beyond required quotas began the new era for business in China. Two years later, special economic zones (SEZs) were created in which market capitalism, development based on foreign investment, export-driven manufacturing, and Chinese-foreign joint ventures (JVs) were allowed to flourish. With the economic growth created by these measures, resources became available to improve China's infrastructure. Modern electrical plants, power lines, highways, railroads, ports, and communication lines were built, creating a new cycle of opportunities for business. This period also saw the creation of institutional foundations for development, such as stock exchanges, commercial laws, and a re-opening of universities. Over 100 new special economic zones were eventually created, and foreign firms were allowed to operate in most cities, increasing exports to almost 40 percent of GDP. Privately owned, market-oriented businesses were allowed to form in most industries, increasing the private share of GDP to nearly 70 percent (comparable to many Western nations). State-owned enterprises, allowed greater autonomy and greater incentives, were converted to shareholder ownership and offered to investors via listings on domestic and foreign stock exchanges.

FINDING OPPORTUNITIES AS CHINA'S MARKETS DEVELOP

MARKET STAGE	RISKS FOR BUSINESS	OPPORTUNITIES	WINNING STRATEGY
Greenfield— product and market uncertain	Betting on unproven demand	Matching the new industry with company advantage	Get there first, grow most rapidly
Fragmented, immature market; growing market, many products	Decreasing margins as competitors crowd in	Acquiring failing competitors	Gain market share, be flexible and agile
Consolidation phase; emerging product standards	Losing advantage	Setting industry design standards	Be a fast-follower, first to economic scale
Mature market; standard product with inter- changeable parts	Incremental loss of advantage	Creating a new game, while staying ahead in the old game	Create efficient process for repeated innovation
Post-mature, shrinking market; outdated products not replaced	Being affected by decline or stagnation	Find new markets and new products	Shift business to fast- growth developing markets

Moving the goalposts

*China price— *a recognized term for the lowest price globally, frequently 30–50 percent below the price in Europe or the US.*

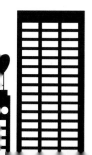

China's first efforts at free enterprise were based on low-technology, labor-intensive manufacturing at a very low price. But today, Chinese engineers and entrepreneurs are capable of manufacturing very sophisticated products, almost without limit, at a "China price"* that can beat the prices in world markets by up to 70 percent. The trend—and the explicit national plan—for the basis of future competition is innovation in design, technology, content, and branding—a transition, if you like, from "Made in China" to "Invented in China." In other words, Chinese firms intend to become more like Western ones, and foreign firms doing business there need to work hard to achieve a sustainable advantage.

"China, Inc." today

The rapid and dramatic transformation in China's economic and business landscape is virtually unprecedented, yet the legacy of what went before still permeates all areas of business in China today. The accelerated rate of transition in what is still a collectivist and intensely bureaucratic culture has given rise to some uniquely Chinese business practices and positions.

TIP

ARMY RETREAT
If you last visited China before 1998, you may be surprised today not to see the once widespread Peoples' Liberation Army (PLA)-operated businesses, which ranged from the manufacture of military supplies to the operation of hotels, horse races, coal mines, and karaoke parlors. Many of these firms still exist, but most are no longer directly PLA-owned.

Residual central planning

Companies that, before 1978, were arms of central or local government have largely been converted to share ownership corporations, and many are now listed on international stock exchanges. Despite progress in converting China's economy to full market orientation, the state often remains the largest shareholder, directly or indirectly influencing corporate decisions. Banks may lend funds to achieve important government policies, such as environmental protection, worker safety, energy conservation, or rural investment, with little regard to profitability or shareholder value. Manufacturers may limit price increases to help the government combat inflation. State-owned suppliers may preferentially provide scarce raw materials to state-owned manufacturers. Firms with a long history in an area may decide to retain unneeded workers, unprofitable facilities, or special worker benefits.

CASE STUDY

A legacy of compliance
State-owned firms are essentially autonomous with regard to day-to-day operations, but will often respond to specific requests from the government, usually designed to further social policy. The results of such willingness to cooperate can, to outsiders, appear extraordinary. For example, in 2004 the CEOs of China Telecom, China Unicom, and China Mobile agreed, at the request of the government, to exchange their positions, each becoming CEO of a competing firm.

Hypercompetition

Most Chinese industries are fragmented into many small companies, none large enough to compete effectively globally. By 2008, China was home to 37 cell phone companies, 120 car manufacturers, 8,000 software companies, 10,000 auto parts manufacturers, 18,000 freight companies and 3PL* providers, and 94,000 book printers. This pattern, of many small companies, is also true for the home appliance, consumer electronics, beer brewing, clothing and fashion, toy, steel, and many other industries.

3PL—third party logistics. 3PL providers are typically firms offering outsourced warehousing and distribution systems customized to their clients' business needs.

Often these tiny firms compete mainly on price rather than on brand, quality, product design, unique technology, or reliable delivery. Let the buyer beware! China's fragmented markets present the foreign businessperson with a chaotic and rapidly changing environment where almost anything can be manufactured, often at prices that seem too good to be true.

Working with local protectionism

Many Chinese local governments are major shareholders in local companies, and most senior government officials are judged, to a large degree, on the economic growth in their local area. These two facts provide a strong incentive for officials to protect and support local firms, often at the expense of firms from other cities, provinces, and nations.

Protectionism may take the form of licensing fees, vague and protracted certification processes, "buy local" incentives, local government purchasing contracts, and city and provincial customs inspections. If you want to do business throughout China, it may be necessary to establish duplicate facilities in many of the major provinces and cities in order to establish credentials as a "local" firm in each individual region.

Recognizing business types

China's business environment is complex, including domestic firms, joint ventures, and wholly foreign-owned enterprises. The various types of domestic Chinese firms interact very differently with foreign business people. Determine what type of Chinese business you are dealing with before trying to form a business relationship.

TIP

PARTNER WITH A UNIVERSITY
Consider Chinese universities as potential business partners. Universities in China actually own and operate many corporations, in fields such as software engineering, semiconductor design, medicine, and structural and civil engineering.

State-owned enterprises

State-owned "policy firms" or SOEs, such as railroads, China's TV network, universities, development banks, aircraft manufacture industries, and airports, exist primarily to implement important social programs and to support major government policies—although they also want to make money. In 2003, it was estimated that just over half of China's SOEs were loss-making, but recent reforms have been vigorously aimed at improving efficiency and profitability.

Former SOEs

Formerly state-owned enterprises that now operate autonomously for profit may be listed on Chinese and foreign stock exchanges. The state is usually a major shareholder. Mostly market-oriented, they have rapidly adopted many of the best practices of foreign competitors. While needing to achieve profitability, they often retain some of their previous social agenda, and will usually respond to specific policy requests from the government.

Collectives

Township and village collective enterprises (TVEs) were originally designed to provide employment opportunities for local—usually rural—citizens. Agriculture is a major area of operation, although they also manufacture consumer goods. Collectives are generally very market-oriented and flexible, and some are emerging as global competitors. This type of firm is relatively very productive.

Private enterprises

Completely private enterprises owned by Chinese individuals have little policy agenda beyond a desire to exhibit good citizenship. They include many manufacturing firms, especially trade-related ones. The best are often led by returning Chinese with advanced degrees from top foreign universities and experience of working within leading Western companies.

Joint ventures

In Chinese–foreign joint ventures, the Chinese partner is usually a state-owned firm. While foreign technology, management skills, and financing combine with inside knowledge of China to create a major market force, the partners' goals and methods may conflict.

Non-Chinese firms

Wholly foreign-owned firms— subsidiaries or divisions of global firms—are currently the favored investment model, creating 85 percent of China's electronics exports, 70 percent of its plastics exports, and 60 percent of its equipment exports. Foreign "contract firms" source components and finished goods in China, specifying designs and often equipment and operating procedures to suppliers. Foreign "transactional firms" buy Chinese raw materials, components, or finished goods for export and sale abroad, without specifying design or participating in the manufacturing process.

Reaching out to China's consumers

The many different faces of China manifest themselves in very distinctive consumer types, some unique to China. Urban and rural markets, markets in different regions, groups of consumers distinguished by their age and gender, and consumers with fixed attitudes toward marketing require very different approaches when doing business in China.

Urban and rural markets

Rural consumers—two-thirds of the population—tend to be at an earlier stage in the cycle of consumerism, working to acquire the first four requirements for "well off" status: a bicycle, TV, refrigerator, and phone. Rural residents are more likely to buy on sight rather than after study, are much less aware of brands, and are extremely price-sensitive. Purchases are likely to be short-term consumables. City-dwellers, on the other hand, are more sophisticated consumers—aware of both domestic and foreign brands and responsive to advertising—who study their options ahead of time. With three times the disposable income they are more likely to buy expensive durable goods based on value.

CULTURAL ANTENNAE

Branded goods

Consumers in China often use purchases to signal social status. With highly visible products such as clothing, watches, cars, cigarettes, and homes, they are more likely to purchase a costly brand over a functionally identical discount brand. Foreign brands are highly regarded, not only for their prestige value but also because they are perceived to have much higher quality. Introducing a branded product into China can be very rewarding, if affordability and trademark protection issues are addressed. Before introducing your brand in China, make sure you register your trademark with the Chinese Trademark Office. Also choose a Chinese name for the brand, checking carefully that it has no negative phonetic, historical, or luck-related interpretations.

TIP

**UNDERSTAND
THE MENTALITY**
Online purchasing
has been relatively
slow to take off in
China, partly
because payment
options have been
slow to develop, and
partly due to
widespread suspicion
of fraud. Face-to-face
transactions endure,
so buyers and sellers
can be sure that they
are getting what
they expected.

Age and gender differences

Chinese men aged between 30 and 45 often buy on the instructions of a wife or child. Their purchases tend to be for their own use and the decision is likely to be based on utility. Women aged between 30 and 45 make some 70 percent of the purchases for the whole family, and traditionally manage the savings and financial services for the household. These consumers tend to buy based on value (quality at a reasonable price) and convenience.

Retired people, many of whom live with younger family members, tend to be less active purchasers who exhibit very low personal consumption, except for health care, cameras, TVs, and travel. A low average retirement age and the phenomenon of single-child families has made this a rapidly growing segment of the Chinese population.

The "little emperor" syndrome

Children in China are very active influencers. The single child family rule has created a unique market segment popularly known as "little emperors." Each of these children may be the focus of the attention of two parents, four grandparents, and numerous aunts and uncles. They carry a great deal of weight in decisions regarding educational products, toys, fast food, and entertainment. Little emperors often decide based on advertising.

7%
"TRUST WORD OF MOUTH"
Older, retired workers, mostly lower-income, who ignore advertisements and promotions, but are loyal to familiar brands and may base buying decisions on the opinions of friends.

8%
"BUY IT ON SALE"
Blue-collar workers, mostly over the age of 55, who see little difference between brands but do respond promotions.

Assessing regional differences

Of course, each region of China is comprised of many different types of people, but when you visit Beijing, Shanghai, and Shenzhen you may, if you are attuned to such things, notice a very different type of consumer culture.

• **Beijing** The capital is home to a wide range of types of consumer, including many government officials, diplomats, foreign and domestic corporate managers, and university and high-technology researchers. Books, computers, imported goods, and luxury products are well received. According to surveys, Beijing consumers are relatively more motivated by product quality.

21%
"LET'S TRY IT"
Higher-income office and managerial workers who are sensitive to brand positioning and frequently switch brands. This category includes more women than men, and is dominated by middle-aged consumers.

26%
"STAND BY YOUR BRAND"
Younger, socially active workers who respond to promotions and are loyal to major brands. An attitude most commonly seen in Shanghai and by workers employed by foreign firms.

38%
"JUST SAY NO"
Older, less socially active, government and state-owned enterprise workers who dislike advertising and are not motivated by brands. An attitude especially prevalent in Beijing.

- **Shanghai** This is regarded as China's most cosmopolitan and international city, with the highest disposable income of any region of China. Market research reveals that Shanghai is home to a unique market segment made up of affluent and very socially active women. Shanghainese buy a lot more of everything, especially luxury goods, beauty products, household appliances, health products, and on-line purchases. Surveys have discovered that people in Shanghai rely on the recommendations of friends in making purchase decisions.

- **Shenzhen** Shenzhen is part of the very entrepreneurial South, home to many generations of traders and merchants. Shenzhen and the surrounding area is the source of much of China's clothing, furniture, home appliances, and computers, so these products are widely available at low prices. Perhaps as a result, consumers are especially motivated to purchase products that will signal their affluence, and are more receptive to top brands and imported prestige goods.

Understanding politics

The Chinese government is currently very welcoming to business, technology, and research, and to positive relationships internationally. Interacting with the local ministries and agencies can, at times, require patience and good humor, but once you have proven a good corporate citizen, government officials will become your most important allies.

TIP

MAKE FRIENDS
After you establish a basic relationship with a government official, suggesting they visit your firm or home in your country can help foster beneficial relations. It can also lead to genuine friendship.

Getting to grips with red tape

Chinese government is composed of three branches: the executive branch, led by the President and Premier, and administered by the State Council through a complex bureaucracy; the legislative branch, led by the single-house National Peoples' Congress (which studies and enacts the law, and elects the President and Vice-president); and the judicial branch, led by the Supreme Peoples' Court.

This structure is generally replicated on the provincial level and, for the executive and judicial branches, on the municipal level. Paralleling the government structure at each of these levels is the Communist Party organization, with a municipal General Secretary filling a position that is effectively comparable to that of a town's mayor.

CULTURAL ANTENNAE

Avoiding political pitfalls
In dealing with Chinese business people and government officials, a high level of sensitivity is necessary when discussing:
- Taiwan, Tibet, Hong Kong, and Macau as parts of China
- Chinese–Japanese interaction 1936–1945
- The 1989 occurrences in Tiananmen Square (and civil disorder in general)
- Mao Zedong or other founders of China

- Religion in general
- Trade unions and workers' rights
- The convertibility and value of Chinese currency
- International trade disputes, and the actions of the WTO
- The role of Communism in China's economy
- Perceived failures of socialism in history
- The relative merits of liberal democracy.

Business people normally interact most frequently with municipal leaders, such as the mayor and multiple vice-mayors, and with the local offices of the State Council ministries, such as the Ministry of Science and Technology, the Ministry of Commerce, or the State Administration for Industry and Commerce. These local offices are funded by local government, and while they nominally report to Beijing, they often seem more influenced by the agendas and priorities of local government. This can be beneficial if you have a local project to implement, but frustrating for a firm wanting to create a national organization. The key to dealing with government in China is transparency and good corporate citizenship. They will be watching to see that, while you are making generous profits, you also care about the welfare of your Chinese workers and of the community and will support the important social objectives of the nation, such as investment in rural areas and energy conservation.

TIP

AVOID THE MIDDLEMEN
The overlapping and competitive nature of Chinese ministries often necessitates multiple visits to get something done. There are agents and expediters who will volunteer to "take care of all the details" but since these encounters with bureaucracy are relatively infrequent but important, it may be wiser to simply get in line.

FOSTERING GOOD RELATIONS

FAST TRACK	**OFF TRACK**
Demonstrating your commitment to China symbolically by contributing to charitable or cultural organizations	Mixing an agenda for political or social change with your business aims in China
Employing patience and good humor in dealing with the bureaucracy	Complaining about inevitable bureaucratic delays—China invented bureaucracy
Cultivating long-term and trusting relationships with government officials	Attempting to influence officials with lavish gifts, entertainment, or cash

Finding the opportunities

Business people in China are achieving remarkable success by selling very ordinary products, as well as through the two almost universal routes: property and the stock market. The demands of the growing middle class, the urgent needs of rapidly expanding industries, and the continuing cycle of development all offer excellent opportunities.

Using established paths

What industries have so far provided the biggest rewards? Household appliances, food flavorings, computer games, car parts, animal feed, grocery and hardware retail, fertilizer, and fire-safety products have all created remarkable recent fortunes in China, as have those traditional tools of the very rich outside China—chemical manufacture, property development, pharmaceuticals, and the stock market.

And while the early opportunities for enterprise in low-tech manufacturing are mostly long gone, one steady path to wealth in China is providing inputs needed by other firms to create consumer goods and services. From agriculture to manufacturing and financial services, China's growth requires mundane raw materials, services, components, and supplies. Do you make a better shipping container, or software to manage human resources effectively? Business-to-business opportunities in China might be right for you.

FORTUNES MAY RESIDE IN THE ORDINARY

Emerging hotspots

China's greatest opportunities are perhaps still in waiting. In industry, the focus has now shifted to cutting-edge technology. The way forward lies in advanced Western medicine, biotechnology, nanotechnology, and new materials, and the environmental protection and alternative energy industries, together with technical consulting.

There are growing opportunities in catering to China's emergent middle class. Some 250 million Chinese are beginning to demand all the products and services that a better life implies. Education is a top cultural priority, and includes basic foreign language, technical, and business education. Convenience food and beverages and do-it-yourself stores are all major growth industries. The infant financial services industry in China is also ripe for development.

ASK YOURSELF... WHERE'S OUR BUSINESS NICHE?

- What unique knowledge or abilities does my firm possess that can be translated into a desirable product or service in China?
- How can my firm's capabilities and products be reconfigured to adapt to Chinese markets?
- What niche market in my industry is least well served in China?
- How can my company transform an initial cost advantage in China into a long-term, well-defended competitive advantage?
- What government policies can give my venture extra momentum?
- What unique business model (method of delivering value to target customers) will provide an advantage in China?
- Which Chinese products would my existing customers value?
- What components or other business inputs would be advantageously sourced in China?

CASE STUDY

Mrs. Zhang's paper fortune

Chinese paper, made from straw or bamboo fiber, is poor quality and relatively expensive. Or at least it was until Los Angeles resident Yin Zhang recognized the challenge and the opportunity. Environmental laws in the US and Europe created a vast but mostly unwanted supply of waste paper intended for recycling, while China lacked the large forests to supply the packing boxes, copy paper, and household paper products demanded by its growing economy. Mrs. Zhang saw an opportunity in simultaneously solving both problems by connecting them. Her Nine Dragons Paper Company, which converts recycled paper from abroad into boxes, packaging, and household paper products for China, now has an annual revenue of over one billion dollars.

Chapter 2
Understanding business etiquette

In China, business is governed by long-term relationships, so understanding business etiquette is essential to understanding the Chinese business culture. If you only have time to read one chapter in this book, make sure you read this one.

Respecting social conventions

In China, many unique and rigid rules govern all forms of socializing. Compounding this difficulty, after-hours socialization is the primary method of creating business opportunities and solving business problems. So it is important to understand the rules.

Following basic rules of conduct

Friends and associates in China may readily forgive minor social gaffes, but failing to follow one basic rule will cause unending trouble: always treat the people you meet with respect, interest, and restrained, semi-formal good humor. This type of conduct is not seen as cold, weak, or patronizing, but as dignified, sincere, and cultured. In addition, modesty is almost always appreciated more than exaggerated gestures, modes of speech, or opinions. Bear in mind that the Chinese people tend to be patriotic, so knowledge of history and culture, and respect for it, is graciously received.

TIP

Taking cues from the Chinese

KEEP YOUR DISTANCE

While the normal distance between people during conversation is smaller in China than in the West, touching another person's arm, hugging, gripping a shoulder, or back-slapping are considered extremely rude—unless you are in northeast China near the Russian border, where all foreigners receive a "Russian welcome."

Many of the social conventions treasured in other countries are unfamiliar to the Chinese. One example is the concept of waiting in line: in China, the pattern for a waiting crowd is not linear but circular, spreading outward from the focus of attention like ripples in a pond. Another convention infrequently seen in China is the practice of egalitarianism, where business, social, or economic inferiors are treated with a show of casual friendliness. Urban China is more hierarchical than that, and rich or powerful people are expected to look and act accordingly.

In public, shows of emotion are not welcome, which extends to smiling, and expressing gratitude or disappointment. And while classmates, friends, and family members of the same gender are often physically affectionate in public, even minor displays of affection in public by couples is considered offensive. If you are traveling with a partner, be aware, too, that it will not be appropriate for them to attend all social functions. In a country where business relationships are forged and deals negotiated not in boardrooms or law offices but at dining tables, in karaoke clubs, and on golf courses, "business as usual" continues well after hours.

CULTURAL ANTENNAE

Tolerating behavioral customs

Certain behaviors that are perfectly normal in China can startle the visitor. Your Chinese associates may spit in public, for example, as traditionally this is seen as health-promoting. Talking with the mouth full or making loud "lip-smacking" noises while eating is the Chinese way of showing enthusiasm for a meal, and smoking during meals and in confined spaces is widespread. Foreigners are also often disconcerted by the Chinese flexibility with regard to schedules, rules, and laws (the latter especially so when driving) but again, try to retain your composure.

What you can do is avoid some "typical" foreign behaviors that irritate Chinese people: pointing, or summoning with the index finger (use an open hand); showing the soles of your shoes (keep them facing the floor); wearing shoes in private homes (considered unhygienic), and making vivid facial expressions and exaggerated gestures while speaking.

Getting social etiquette right

Sharing conversation, meals, drinks, and entertainment is central to building relationships, and therefore central to doing business in China. A willingness to engage in the quite complex protocols that govern social engagements in China says to your Chinese hosts, "I respect you".

EXCHANGE BUSINESS CARDS
Offer and receive business cards with both hands, taking a moment to study the card before putting it away. Offer business cards oriented so that they can be read by the recipient without turning. Make every effort to remember names and pronunciation.

Making introductions

Avoid self-introductions. For important contacts, take the time to arrange an introduction by a trusted associate of your desired contact. Show respect by standing while the introduction takes place, if at all possible. The introduction may be followed by a handshake and an exchange of cards. In either case, wait for the other person to initiate the action. Avoid over-familiarity such as touching, using first names, showing emotion, or giving over-the-top compliments. The ideal attitude for conversation is restrained friendliness, tempered by modesty and sincerity.

AVOID "UNLUCKY" GIFTS
Avoid gifts that relate to time, the number four, umbrellas, writing in red ink, scissors or knives, white paper or flowers, and everyday food items, as they may convey unintended negative messages.

Choosing gifts

Gifts that reflect the interests of both the giver and recipient are best. Photographic books on your home region or delicacies for which it is famous are usually good choices. Gifts are often declined several times before they are accepted, so mild persistence may be required. If the refusal seems unusually strong or enduring, it may be real. Gifts are usually not opened at the time they are received. Very lavish gifts should be avoided for two reasons. In business or government contexts they may be considered bribes. In all contexts, the recipient is expected to eventually reciprocate with a comparable gift, which will cause embarrassment if that is economically impossible.

Dining

Seating at any meal should follow rank. As a guest, wait for your host to indicate a seat. When hosting a dinner, choose the middle seat opposite the room's entrance for yourself, and invite your most senior guest to sit on your left, the next most senior on your right. Seat the rest of the group according to position, the most junior attendees nearest the door.

• As a host, it is good form to begin the meal by suggesting a toast, then serving your guest of honor. After this formality, guests serve themselves.

• As a guest, try a bit of each dish presented, however unappealing. Some of the most startling dishes you will see are expensive delicacies in China.

• Dishes at Chinese banquets are shared from a rotating platform in the center of the table. As a host, make certain that enough food and drink is served, with a considerable margin, to completely satisfy all your guests.

• If you are not adept with chopsticks, practice using them ahead of time. Try to avoid putting the ends of your chopsticks in your mouth, standing them upright in food, waving them around, or dropping them. When using the toothpicks normally provided, cover your mouth with one hand.

• Offering and accepting toasts is a normal part of dining and relationship building, so be sure to participate. It is acceptable to toast with soft drinks or fruit juice if you want to avoid alcohol. You can claim a health condition if offers of the very potent white "wine" are persistent.

• The arrival of a plate or platter of watermelon, or other fruit, signals the end of the meal. As a guest, at the end of the meal always leave some food on your plate as a sign that you are satisfied.

Succeeding with guanxi

A vast network reaching every corner of China, guanxi is the engine that drives Chinese business, and is essential for both local and foreign business people. Understanding, building, and using guanxi is probably the most important task facing foreigners in China.

> **Guanxi linkages connect most or all of the business people in China in a vast human network.**

LEARN TO SAY IT
"Guanxi" is pronounced "gwan" (as in guano) + "she", spoken with a level (neither rising nor falling) tone.

Defining guanxi?

Guanxi is a relationship of deep understanding, feeling, trust, and respect, sustained by a moral obligation to preserve the relationship, and a need to maintain one's personal honor and status within the relationship. The closest relationships of trust, understanding, and obligation are always with family members. More distant relatives, close friends, school classmates, and home town neighbours form a second tier. Newer friends, business associates, members of one's trade group, and similar acquaintances form a third level. Residents in one's home town, alumni of the same university, and other similar "undiscovered friends" form a more tenuous fourth level. Self-introduced strangers form a last level at which essentially no guanxi is present.

Guanxi is a tool that has been developed for a specific purpose: to create high-trust situations in a generally low-trust environment. Guanxi relationships are dynamic, strengthening every time they are successfully used, and weakening as their use fails.

> **Levels of guanxi affect the amount of resources the person providing the service is willing to expend, as well as the likelihood of the request being granted at all.**

Some characteristics of guanxi

Benefits provided via guanxi relationships are not expected to be entirely symmetrical or connected in time. The service you receive may require very costly reciprocation years later.

Guanxi is connected to the person, not the business or institution, and is not transferable.

Guanxi relationships take a long time to develop and are permanent rather than part of a transaction.

A business person ostracized for ignoring guanxi obligations may find it very difficult to function.

Guanxi is very different from corruption, although there is a fine line between the two.

Guanxi does not guarantee that a person's desires will be fulfilled, only that they are known and will be considered when the decision is made.

MAKE CONNECTIONS INDIRECTLY

Introductions by strangers have little positive value in China. Use a guanxi network to connect via the person's trusted circle of friends, and you are more than halfway toward your business objective. Connecting through a friend of a friend of a friend may be time-consuming but the results will handsomely reward the effort.

Saving costs with guanxi

Guanxi networks fill many of the functions that credit agencies, contracts, and courts fill in Western societies—performing background checks and verifying credentials, regulating personal conduct, and resolving disputes. In China, until very recently, few of these options were available, but there was still a need to manage the risk of business relationships. Guanxi networks assure the conduct of individuals, allow social and sometimes material resources to be allocated efficiently, and provide avenues for dispute resolution and a means of punishment for unacceptable behavior.

Guanxi plays a major role in "the China price." Businesses in a guanxi society save on costs regarded as normal in a legalistic society—for example, lawyers' fees on both sides of any transaction, allowances for credit-reporting fees, business insurance, legal costs, adverse publicity, and court judgments—and these savings are passed on to the customer.

In no sense is guanxi seen as bribery, nepotism, or corruption. It is just a different approach to managing uncertainty and risk.

Joining up to the network

Business goals and strategies often require social and other resources that are outside your direct control. The Chinese guanxi "internet" is China's solution to this dilemma, and can work for you if you are prepared to put in the time and effort to cultivate your own guanxi (see overleaf). Guanxi networks connect every part of China and, with a few intermediate connections, can potentially link you to all the nation's business people. If you have a business that needs to expand to China, why ignore a network that can connect you to 1.3 billion decision-makers, suppliers, and customers there?

HOW GUANXI COMPARES WITH WESTERN NETWORKING

WESTERN NETWORKING	GUANXI
Built on legal system	Built on social-moral system
The start of a business relationship	The start of a friendship
Self introduction	Introduced
Simple and direct	Complex and subtle
Deep feelings not appropriate	Need for close human feeling
Can be quick and one-time-based	Requires patience and a long-term view
Knowing someone means a lot	Knowing someone might mean nothing
Conductive way of thinking	Deductive way of thinking

TIP

WAIT TO BE INTRODUCED
Chinese guanxi works in the West, but Western-style up-front networking techniques are rarely appropriate in China. For example, always wait to be introduced by your host to a potential new associate—don't take the lead yourself.

Using the guanxi network

While guanxi is not Western networking, it can be used in similar ways. It must be mutually beneficial: that is, used both for your own needs and to secure favors for your guanxi contacts—for example, an introduction to a powerful official or potential client, a position or promotion at work, a slot in a graduate or research program, or access to a scarce resource. Guanxi can help you find reliable business partners and suppliers, create new customers, discover opportunities, and obtain hard-to-find information.

Guanxi is "spent" by making a friend aware of a situation you are concerned about, and perhaps asking for advice. If the relationship is sufficiently strong, the friend may decide to dedicate the very considerable effort of engaging his or her own guanxi network on your behalf. This can be a major undertaking with serious consequences, as the friend is essentially guaranteeing your character and reliability. Do not be too disappointed if they cannot solve your problem.

Creating your guanxi network

How does a foreigner create what seems to be a uniquely Chinese social structure? You probably already have the beginnings of a guanxi network without realizing it, via friends, classmates, colleagues, professional services providers, and long-time neighbors.

TIP

BORROW FROM THE BEST
Rather than create your entire guanxi network from the ground up, tap into top-quality branches around you. Chinese who have returned to China after studying and working in the West often have remarkable guanxi networks, notable both for their size and for the influential people that connect to it. Officials at your regional Chinese Embassy are a treasure hoard of guanxi and it is their job to link you to it.

Mobilizing your forces

Review your existing contacts: a cousin working for a multinational in Shanghai who knows officials there; a close friend whose college roommate from Wuhan could provide useful introductions. A favorite retailer that imports some stock from China could put you in contact with a reliable trading company. Most medium to large Western cities have sister-city relationships with Chinese cities; this can yield excellent high-level introductions. The Asian studies department of your local university or alma mater may contain scores of well-connected Chinese students.

Making successful connections

Most importantly, when building a guanxi network, be selective. The reliability and positions of your friends and associates determine your attractiveness as a potential member of a wider network.

Secondly, connect to guanxi networks via high-level introductions. An introduction by a high-level official or company CEO is likely to succeed, while strangers introducing themselves and introductions arranged by low-level employees have little positive value.

Thirdly, be opportunistic. Opportunities to quietly smooth over a contact's mistake, allocate credit for a success to an associate, or solve a problem for a colleague can gain you instant access to a network.

Cultivating guanxi

Guanxi relationships are long-term, essentially permanent, and require nurturing and maintenance.

• Most importantly, be sure to guard your reputation and the respect of your acquaintances and friends in China.

• Remember to spend enjoyable time with your guanxi network members regularly. Recreation, a meal, shopping, a special event, or a conversation over tea or coffee are all excellent tools for maintaining the relationship.

• Share other parts of your own network with your Chinese contacts. Foreigners can very effectively maintain guanxi by inviting Chinese friends to visit their home and family abroad. Delivering opportunities is a guanxi builder.

• Remember the sources of your successes. If an introduction or resource creates a profitable new venture, include the friend who made the introduction or provided the resource in its success.

• Show contacts you appreciate them as people. Learning about their family, hobbies, major life experiences, and values is a guanxi builder, as is memorizing their likes and dislikes. Small gifts related to their interests are an effective way to tell Chinese friends that they are valued.

HOW TO... NURTURE YOUR NETWORK

Print business cards with Chinese on one side and your native language on the other.

↓

Ask a trusted Chinese friend to help you choose an appropriate Chinese name.

↓

Make the effort to learn at least a few key phrases in Chinese—a little work can make a big impression even if you never become fluent.

↓

Dive into China's nightlife, taking every opportunity to make valuable friends.

↓

Take every opportunity to help solve problems for Chinese associates.

↓

Go to great lengths to avoid embarrassing potential contacts.

↓

Be creative in avoiding potential conflicts; solve problems at the earliest possible stage.

↓

Discover common areas that can form a bridge to trust.

↓

Keep a journal recording every gift received, so that you can reciprocate consistently and appropriately.

Maintaining guanxi

While building guanxi can take many years, a single major mistake can completely destroy these trust-based connections. If you abuse your guanxi relationships through neglect or bad manners, or attempt to exploit them, doors may become permanently closed to you.

TIP

RECOGNIZE APPROACHES

You will rarely be asked directly for a favor or service by a guanxi contact. You are more likely to be indirectly provided with information about a concern, or requested advice, which signals an opportunity for you to cultivate guanxi. You need to become adept at recognizing these discreet approaches if your guanxi is to prosper.

Avoiding "guanxi killers"

A lack of respect—for China and Chinese culture, for the reputation and personal feelings of your Chinese contacts, or for the mutuality of your relationship with them—is the root cause of many common "guanxi killers." Be sure you are never guilty of:

• Not delivering on promises; failing to provide or reciprocate favors
• Introducing someone who damages your reputation
• Aggressively or immodestly selling yourself
• Impatience in seeing results; demanding quid pro quo
• Always asking, seldom giving; greed
• Not sharing other parts of your network with Chinese contacts
• "Disappearing" until something is needed
• Complaining
• Pointing out the mistakes of others
• Claiming undeserved credit for an accomplishment
• Failing to express thanks in concrete terms
• Creating situations requiring serious apologies
• Not passing on information that could be important to a contact, because it is not tied to any request.

Steering clear of corruption

Because creating and using guanxi is central to doing business in China, understanding the line between guanxi and corruption is vitally important. Crossing it may lead to devastating consequences. Personal embarrassment, career termination, fines and imprisonment, and negative publicity for your firm are just a few of the possible results. For Chinese officials, large-scale corruption violations, including giving and receiving bribes, embezzlement, failing to report large gifts, hiding unlawful profits, and corruption-related tax evasion, are subject to the death penalty.

As we have seen, guanxi is a long-term personal relationship of trust, affection, and reciprocated favors. Corruption, on the other hand, is the failure to perform a recognized duty properly, based on intended personal benefit.

So when is "guanxi" corruption? The key issue is whether or not the favors that are given violate a duty to someone else. In our work we may owe a duty to advance the interests of our employers, our shareholders, our clients, or, if we are public officials, the community and nation. Providing a favor for a member of our guanxi network that violates any of our duties to others is corruption, which is both unethical and illegal.

CASE STUDY

Identifying corruption
Suppose you hope to sell a product to a Chinese firm. After a few dinners and an evening of karaoke with the buyer for the firm, the buyer implies a willingness to reveal the details of the other bids in order to let you win. He or she suggests you divide the extra profit equally. Is this corruption or normal Chinese guanxi? The answer is that while it is perhaps disguised as guanxi, this is corruption, pure and simple. There are no deep personal feelings or long-term commitment. There is a clear intent to violate one's duties to others in order to acquire personal benefit. Such a suggestion should be unambiguously declined.

Managing "face" and image

"Face" is an aspect of Chinese business culture that may not be readily apparent at first, but is vitally important. Understanding what face is, defending it in oneself, and ensuring it for your business contacts will bring you a great deal closer to success in China.

Understanding face

In China, face combines one's social status or prestige, and one's reputation for integrity and morality. It is the image you project and the status you claim in society. Building or saving face means projecting an image of goodness, competence, and strength. Social position, respect, and personal honor are very important in China, so your personal image and your effect on the image of those you meet are key to your success.

Saving, giving, and losing face

In practice, almost every conversation you engage in involves a negotiation of face between participants. Do your actions and ideas imply high personal honor and rank for yourself? If so, you are saving face. Do your ideas and proposals implicitly enhance the honor and prestige of the person you are speaking with and his or her organization? If so, you are giving face. Knowing how this works is essential to working with Chinese people. In their hierarchical culture, people in general only deal seriously with those they perceive to be of higher or similar rank. Loss of face can cut you off from the contacts most important to success; you may be perceived as undesirable or unreliable—an unsuitable business partner. Should you cause a business contact to lose a lot of face in an important situation, you may make a permanent enemy.

TACKLE PROBLEM AREAS BEFORE A MEETING
In a discussion or negotiation Chinese business people will attempt to minimize the risk of losing face. They are likely to let the other side know of any non-negotiable positions well ahead of time and will only agree to meet if these positions are acceptable (implicitly or as the result of lower level meetings). If there is too much risk of humiliation and loss of face, the meeting will not occur.

BUILD OR SAVE FACE BY:
- Being seated in a separate, more desirable part of the meeting room (such as behind the podium)
- Employing one or more assistants, translators, drivers, etc.
- Avoiding mundane tasks, such as taking phone calls directly or distributing handouts
- Having (or appearing to have) a full calendar with only limited meeting times available
- Signaling status by using luxury products and services (cars, clothing, hotels, restaurants, etc.).

GIVE FACE TO OTHERS BY:
- Standing while the other person stands, sitting only after he or she is seated
- Minimizing or ignoring the minor errors or failings of others
- Allocating good ideas or achievements to others
- Paying close attention to, and remembering, important details about your business contacts—the ultimate sign of respect and honor.

DON'T LOSE FACE BY:
- Rejection of a social or business proposal
- Receiving a personal criticism in public or private
- Being the subject of contradictory or derogatory remarks
- Arranging meetings which do not implicitly reflect rank and prestige
- Using or providing cheap, poor quality products or services
- Giving in on issues of little substance
- Failing to achieve goals or meet promises
- Revealing a personal defect, weakness, or mistake
- Sustaining loss or damage to a guanxi relationship
- Performing tasks appropriate to those at a lower level.

Understanding collectivism

No society is entirely collectivist or individualistic, but China is essentially collectivist, and this is one of the most challenging aspects of doing business there. It is extremely important to understand the different values and social patterns, and adapt to those differences in practice.

*Collectivism—a political or economic theory advocating collective control, especially over production and distribution of goods. People in a collectivist culture tend to define themselves in terms of their place in the group, defer to group decisions, and place group needs above personal wants.

Exploring collectivist culture

For a person accustomed to an individualist culture, living in or doing business with a collectivist culture involves an attitude adjustment. Collectivism* answers the question, "who am I?" by defining one's identity in terms of group attributes, and answers the question "what is most important?" by giving priority to the goals of the group or community. Values and attitudes that are therefore paramount in China include: high sensitivity to the needs of others; willingness to defend and promote the interests of the group, and also willingness to depend on the abilities and outcomes of the group; quick perception of long-term needs and consequences; respect for social rituals and protocols; and a strong sense of duty.

Building collectivist credentials

In collectivist cultures personal power is strongly influenced by position in a hierarchy. This means that your organization's reputation, your professional affiliations, and your educational and professional credentials are very important in determining your credibility in China. Your contacts in China will try to assess who you are by asking about the groups to which you belong, and may ignore or discount the personal characteristics valued in individualistic cultures, such as merit and accomplishments.

Adapting to collectivist norms

DON'T MISREAD A "YES."...

Chinese people frequently use the word "yes" simply to mean "I hear you," or "I follow what you are saying," to give a harmonious air to a dialogue. Never assume that "yes" means "I agree," or "Let's do it."

Business organizations entering China must adjust practices that work well at home to reflect the different core values of collectivism. For example, preserving group harmony is a highly valued goal in Chinese business, so direct confrontations, blunt honesty, and critical evaluations can reflect poorly on a foreign business person. In individualistic cultures, conflict is seen as a routine part of doing business, whereas in China it is regarded as a serious social failure. Brainstorming sessions, in which proposals are mooted yet few are expected to be implemented, are a common part of Western business. In China they are virtually unheard of: business proposals are made explicit only after they have already been negotiated, indirectly or at a lower level.

Showing that you can fit in

To demonstrate your adaptability to collectivist ideals:
• Avoid voicing strong personal opinions
• Occasionally tell jokes that make fun of yourself
• Don't sell yourself, let your credentials do it for you
• Be aware of peoples' positions in group hierarchies
• Underplay your best ideas
• Prove that you can cooperate effectively
• Show that your organization contributes to society.

CULTURAL ANTENNAE

Stereotypes and discrimination
Your contacts in China may expect more rigid and differentiated gender roles than you are used to, especially when you are dealing with the older generation. At street level, discrimination based on gender, race, national origin, age, and disabilities is unfortunately widespread. While China's leaders have adopted very good anti-discrimination laws and regulations, the change has not yet percolated downward. Discrimination in China almost always favors foreigners, which local people tend to resent.

Minding your language

The Chinese language can be a real barrier to doing business in China, despite the fact that many Chinese people are multilingual. The Chinese language is so different from Western languages that it may give rise to different patterns of thinking, and this influences business in many ways.

TIP

DON'T PUSH IT
Don't be surprised if a Chinese contact you know is able to read and understand some English is reluctant to speak it: he or she may be too anxious to risk making mistakes.

Learning Chinese

Don't count on using your native language in China, even if it is English, which is a popular subject in Chinese higher education. Chinese people that you meet in the course of daily life are usually fluent only in their local dialect. Mandarin is often used in Chinese schools, so most of your business contacts will be able to communicate using it. If you have a chance to learn some spoken Chinese, make sure it is Mandarin.

COMMUNICATING EFFECTIVELY

FAST TRACK	OFF TRACK
Hiring a qualified translator to accompany you in China	Assuming that your Chinese associates will understand you
Translating presentation material into Chinese; arranging for a translation service when addressing groups	Allowing communication failure to lead to business failure
Learning a little Chinese to show your sincere interest in China	Failing to compliment a Chinese person who speaks your language
Smiling, if all else fails	Losing patience or your sense of humor because of a language gap

Thinking in pictures

- Written Chinese is much more uniform than spoken "Chinese" (of which there are 130 different dialects), with the simplified character set in use throughout mainland China, and traditional characters in use in Taiwan. Many Chinese characters are simplified pictures that refer to objects directly, not through the "code" of an alphabet.

- This habit of thinking first about the whole of an idea rather than its parts is reflected in the Chinese approach to business. Language experts suggest that this habit of thought may make thinking about the big picture and its long-term consequences a little more natural.

- Try to learn the Chinese use of visual metaphors and imagery. For example, if your Chinese associate says, "dog chasing mice," she or he is suggesting that the person the remark is directed at should focus on their own business, not that of others.

Chapter 3

Getting things done

The success of your venture will depend on an understanding of Chinese taxes, registration, infrastructure, modes of entry, and many other business fundamentals. This chapter provides a starting point to implementing your business plan for China, but rates, regulations, and restrictions are constantly under review, so always consult a qualified professional.

Knowing the system

Legal issues are a frequent cause of concern to business people, especially in an unfamiliar and frequently changing legal environment such as China. Understanding the fundamentals of Chinese real estate, taxes, contract practices, intellectual property protection, and finance builds a foundation for success in China's markets.

CONSIDER CONSULTANTS

Most global law firms, management consultants, and accounting firms have at least some representation in China. Their expertise can greatly increase your chances of success.

Getting to grips with tax

The taxation regimen in China involves many technical details and is in constant flux. For example, VAT rates have recently varied from 13 to 17 percent depending on the product. Exports were not charged the tax and small businesses paid only a 4 to 6 percent rate. The special incentive tax rates for foreign investment in special economic zones have mostly ended, while the business tax on turnover has recently varied from 3 to 20 percent. Consult a local accountant for guidance on the latest tax situation.

TIP

Understanding property

ENGAGE A LOCAL LAW FIRM

Restrictions on property ownership, use, taxes upon transfer, and other aspects of real estate law change frequently; a Chinese law firm with good international credentials will keep you up to date.

The Chinese constitution now provides protection for individual and company property rights. There are two types of land rights—allocated and granted. Allocated rights are where a state-owned or related organization receives permission to use land indefinitely, usually with an annual fee, but cannot sell it or use it as security. Allocated rights can be cancelled at any time, and should be avoided by foreign investors. Granted land rights are for a definite period of time, usually 70 years for homes, 50 for factories, and 40 for stores and offices, and are available to individuals and companies, including foreigners. They are similar to the renewable ground leases common in Western countries, but haven't yet existed long enough for the renewal provisions to be implemented in practice.

THE CHINESE TAX LANDSCAPE (2008)

BUSINESS TAX TYPE	SPECIFIC TAX	TAX RATE
Taxes on transactions	Value added tax (VAT) on pre-retail transactions	Normally 17 percent; necessities 13 percent
	Consumption or sales tax	3 to 50 percent
	Business tax	3 to 20 percent
Tax on income	Enterprise income tax (EIT)	15 to 33 percent depending on location
Tax on trade	Customs duties	Variable
Capital gains	Real estate	Up to 30 to 60 percent of profits
	Other capital gains	Added to EIT
Passive income	Interest, royalties, etc.	Added to EIT; 10 percent rate for certain situations
Real estate tax	Based on urban property ownership	1.2 percent of original value or 12 percent of rental value

TIP

USE THE SYSTEM
Do not hesitate to take legal action against rights violators—Chinese judges complain that too few foreigners file lawsuits against IP infringers.

Protecting intellectual property

Enforcement of patents, trademarks, copyright, and trade secrets varies from province to province, but is constantly improving. China has a "first to patent" priority rule, so don't wait until your products are on the market—patent everything, especially designs.

Copyrights should be registered to clearly establish ownership, and you should check the records of existing trademark registrations carefully and file in the correct categories. Registered marks and "famous brands" receive adequate protection in China, and the situation is improving. Ask a trusted advisor to help create an appealing Chinese version of your company name and brands, and submit any applications very early (now would be best!).

Trade secrets are difficult to protect through the courts, so a multi-layered IP protection strategy is recommended. Consider modularizing production, and making at least one key element of your product in your home country. Restrict storage, access, and download rights on your network. Implement employee education, contractual protection, and personnel and partner investigation.

CASE STUDY

Intellectual property protection: the software industry

Software was once considered virtually unprotectable in China, where pirate versions of computer applications costing up to $500.00 per copy were sold for ¥15—about $2.00. Several strategies have helped convert this supposedly hopeless situation into a Chinese success story, including incorporating programs into dedicated memory chips; providing software online; distributing applications through government mandated programs; using extensive customizing so that enterprise software was less useful when copied; employing sophisticated online activation procedures; and lowering the price to match Chinese incomes. While these methods may not apply directly to your firm, the intellectual property protection of your products and services in China can usually be improved if you approach these issues with creativity and an open mind.

Working with financial services

China is aggressively reforming its financial sector into Western-style commercial banks, insurance companies, and capital markets. The transition is not complete, and policy considerations sometimes outweigh market-based concerns. It is not always possible for private Chinese firms to receive full service from these institutions, much less foreign-owned companies.

China's financial sector is gradually opening to foreign financial institutions, so if your familiar financial service partners have not already opened offices in Beijing, Shanghai, and Shenzhen, chances are that they will soon. China enjoys an excess of venture capital (VC) funding, and VCs compete aggressively to fund the best business plans, so your start-up might have a better chance in China than at home.

 CHECKLIST USING CONTRACTS

Contracts are enforceable in China through negotiation, mediation, arbitration, or court judgement. Arbitration is given a number of legal advantages and so is the preferred method. When drafting a contract with a Chinese partner, consider the following—you should be able to answer "yes" to every question:

	YES	NO
• Have you checked and verified the ownership, structure, reputation, and solvency, and even the existence of the Chinese partner?	☐	☐
• Have you asked for payment in advance of delivery and requested security and letters of credit?	☐	☐
• Have you specified the method, time, and currency of payments?	☐	☐
• Have you verified that you will be able to convert any Chinese currency into that of your home country?	☐	☐
• Are the provisions of your contract clear of conflicts with local, national, WTO, and your home country's laws and regulations?	☐	☐
• Do powerful Chinese individuals or organizations have a clear interest in the success of your business?	☐	☐

Building a team in China

It may seem unusual that a nation with a population of over 1.3 billion could experience a labor shortage, but that is just the situation in China with regard to skilled workers, technicians, engineers, and managers. Competitive pay, good working conditions, and fringe benefit packages help control rapidly rising turnover rates among employees.

Hiring in China

Once registered, foreign companies can hire Chinese workers through the local Employment Service Center or directly. Each must have an employment contract spelling out the particulars of the job. No workers under the age of 16 can be hired, and hiring 16–18-year-old workers involves special regulations. There are also special regulations governing female employees. After his or her probationary period, an employee is normally required to give 30 days' notice before leaving, but may do so for any reason.

Hiring foreign employees to work within China normally requires a "Z" visa, an employment permit, and a residency certificate. In order to hire foreign staff, the company must demonstrate that their special abilities or experience are not available within the Chinese workforce.

TIP

COMPETE ON BENEFITS
Currently, the most popular fringe benefit offered to top Chinese employees is a concierge service that takes care of household details, so consider including this in your firm's package.

Employment regulation

Under the State Council, the Ministry of Labor and Social Security (MLSS) administers the laws related to recruitment, wages, contracts, working conditions, safety, discipline, etc. As with other State Council organizations, this ministry maintains provincial and municipal level branches that sometimes adopt unique approaches toward resolving local issues.

The working week

The normal working week is five eight-hour days, and work on the sixth and seventh days in the week must be paid at 200 percent of the contract rate. Employer-mandated work over eight hours per day is limited by law, and must be paid at 150 percent of the normal rate. Work on Chinese national holidays must be paid at 300 percent of the base rate.

Redundancy issues

Firing workers in China is not trivial. Workers can be fired during the legal probation period, or for extreme cause thereafter, such as criminal activity, embezzlement, or causing major harm.

If the position no longer exists, and if the employee cannot be retrained into *any* position, a 30-day notice is required.

Only if the employer is in bankruptcy or court-supervised reorganization, or satisfies local MLSS officials that it faces severe financial difficulties, can workers be laid off for budgetary reasons. Any serious disagreements with workers should be solved through negotiation or mediation, if possible. In China, arbitration is mandatory before any labor-related lawsuit can be filed.

IN FOCUS...
MINIMUM WAGES

Each province has its own minimum wage rates, which may vary depending on the industry and the location within the province. For example, in 2008, Gansu Province required full-time wages of at least ¥340, ¥320, or ¥300 per month (¥4080, ¥3840, or ¥3600 per year), depending on the location inside Gansu. For part-time staff there, the hourly rate is multiplied by 1.4. The minimum wage in Shanghai for the same period was ¥690 per month (¥8280 per year), not including social security fees, housing subsidy, or medical allowance. Skilled employees earn much more. An experienced project manager, for example, might earn ¥17,000 per month (¥200,000 per year) or more.

Environmental issues

Despite strong government support for environmental protection, China's anti-pollution laws are still in the early stages of implementation. Foreign companies doing business in China should resist the temptation to trim pollution control investments, and instead build their reputation and their brand by taking high-profile leadership in "green" practices.

TIP

SEEK OUT GREEN OPPORTUNITIES
With assurances of full government support, both environmental protection and green technologies and products are emerging as a growth areas for foreign entrepreneurs in China.

Polluted cities

According to World Bank estimates, 760,000 Chinese people die prematurely from pollution each year, and, of the world's 20 most polluted cities, China is home to 16. Already short of productive farmland, each year China loses close to 1,000 square miles of agricultural land to desertification. In the drive to feed its huge population and the rush to industrialize, previous generations have disregarded the environment. However, China's current leaders are very focused on correcting these environmental problems, and have enacted comprehensive anti-pollution laws.

Externalized costs

Extremely competitive global markets reward firms that can deliver the lowest possible price. The relatively weak enforcement of environmental laws in China has encouraged both domestic and foreign firms to push a portion of their costs on to the local communities in the form of pollution. For example, in 2005, 100 tons of benzene spilled into the Songhua River, which polluted the water supply of tens of millions of people in China and in Russia. This incurred a fine of only US$128,000 (the maximum at the time), which is both morally inexcusable and economically unsustainable.

IN FOCUS...
CORPORATE SOCIAL RESPONSIBILITY

Whether your firm builds a factory in China or you buy Chinese-made products through a series of brokers and contract suppliers, it is important for you to know and regularly monitor the environmental protection practices along your supply chain. Ignorance is no excuse in averting a public relations disaster from a revelation in the media of gross pollution (or other misdeeds) on the part of your suppliers.

Targeting foreigners

In driving for rapid change in China's environmental protection, it is often to the advantage of the government and the media to seize upon examples of foreign companies that practise lower levels of environmental protection in China than they do at home. In a tactic called "killing the chicken to frighten the monkeys" they hope to send a strong message to domestic firms by severely punishing foreign polluters. This, of course, can dramatically harm public opinion in those foreign companies' home markets, in addition to sharply restricting their future business in China. Try to build up a complete "healthy ecosystem" for your business that embraces employees, suppliers, customers, local communities, government, investors, and others.

Setting an example

Foreign firms doing business in China should never succumb to the temptation to trim environmental protection costs, endangering their reputation in China and at home. Protecting the environment is one of the areas in which foreign firms in China can usefully demonstrate leadership, setting an example and earning the rewards that flow from a trusted and respected brand. In the same way, your firm can also create a competitive advantage by leadership in worker safety, energy efficiency, water conservation, and local community services.

Infrastructure and logistics

In the past, moving equipment, goods, and people to where they were needed in China was not always easy; once there, electricity, water, and other utilities needed by business were not always present. But logistics and infrastructure are rapidly reaching global quality levels all over China.

ALLOW FOR CONTINGENCY

Until all China's ambitious development schemes are complete, practise cautious inventory management, expect some shipping delays, prepare for occasional utility disruptions, and budget a bit extra for unforeseen transportation costs.

HOLD AN AUCTION

Involve several industrial parks in your negotiations, as they are very competitive and each has wide discretion as to offering desirable foreign companies valuable incentives.

Using transportation

China is extending its high-speed road system to reach over 53,000 miles (85,000 km)—longer than the freeway system of the US, and in much better condition. A budget of US$10 billion per year for the next 30 years will ensure access to even the most remote rural towns. China's high-capacity railroad system is one of the most intensely used in the world and is planned to increase its length by 12,500 miles (20,000 km). Over US$17.5 billion over five years will go to build 50 new airports, move ten existing ones, and expand another 71. Nine out of the world's 20 busiest seaports are in China. The new port at Yangshan near Shanghai will be the world's largest, and will function as an internodal point for the rail, road, and inland waterway network.

NATURAL GAS

Available in most urban centers.

Improving access

China has 53 national technology parks where industry-specific infrastructure is readily available. Almost every Chinese city, large or small, has at least one industrial park with preferential utility access, usually at highly discounted rates. Outside the parks, care is needed to ensure that your firm has reliable access to everything it needs for its business operations.

Utilities in China

POSTAL SERVICE AND EXPRESS DELIVERY

Generally very reliable and rapid. Most global delivery companies maintain full service in China.

POWER SUPPLY

Chinese industrial plants experience fairly frequent electricity disruptions, which need to be accommodated within your firm's plans.

RECYCLED ENERGY

China's traditional neighborhood power-generating plants also produce steam that can be put to heating and industrial uses.

WASTE WATER TREATMENT

Does not exist in every location and often is not used where it does exist.

WATER SUPPLY

Adequate in most places, even in the face of a national water shortage. Industrial facilities should plan on pre-use cleaning and post-use treatment.

TELECOMMUNICATIONS

China has installed an extensive fiberoptics telecom backbone supporting the world's largest population of internet users. Chinese internet users spend nearly 2 billion hours per week online.

Starting a business in China

Starting a business in China means overcoming an array of trivial bureaucratic obstacles, but it is not normally especially challenging. Beyond the formalities, establishing your firm's image and reputation in the community are the key startup objectives.

WORK WITH THE COMMUNITY

It is important that you connect well with the wider community. When difficulties are encountered, as in business they inevitably are, you need to have some local goodwill "in the bank."

Being open in an open market

Based on the percentage of imports and exports to total GDP, China has one of the world's most open economies. While full implementation of all World Trade Organization (WTO) targets for market access has not reached "street level" everywhere, starting a business in China is much easier than it is in many other nations—although it still requires a certain level of determination and patience.

Being open and transparent in your business activities right from the start is important. It will take some time and effort to prove your corporate good citizenship. Each member of your management team and expatriate staff must act as an ambassador, always reflecting your firm's values and intentions.

Taking care of formalities

There is a lot of paperwork involved in starting and registering a new business in China, but it is not terribly expensive or difficult, if taken one item at a time. If your firm is considered especially desirable, or if you have good local relations, a staff member of your industrial park or city might be persuaded to walk you through the process. "Business Entry Consultants" abound, but as a group they have very mixed reputations, so only engage one that is recommended by a trusted associate.

Making a splash

It's vital to plan how your firm will first present itself to the community. An opening ceremony is almost mandatory, attended by your firm's highest leaders, as well as political or business luminaries from your home country, if possible. With high-level attendance assured on the "home side," the "Chinese side" may consent to bring its own political stars to your opening.

Openings attended by mayors, First Secretaries, provincial leaders, and (the best case) nationally prominent personalities have the best chance of doing well as they carry the implicit support of those leaders. Make sure that you invite the media and have a professional to take photos. In China, if you don't have a photo to display, it never really happened.

ASK YOURSELF... ARE WE GOING IN TO WIN?

- Does my firm have the financial strength to do business in or with China for the long term?
- Do the company's top managers have the time to attend fully to the many details of operating a business in or with China?
- Does China want and need the product and service package that my firm offers, or does the local market urgently need a Chinese product?
- How does the product need to be localized to suit Chinese tastes?
- Will my firm be able to offer comprehensive after-sales service to customers?
- How can my firm ensure that it builds a sustainable, competitive advantage in its China-related business?

CHECKLIST REGISTER A NEW FIRM WITH:

	YES	NO
• The State Administration for Industry and Commerce	☐	☐
• The Quality and Technology Supervision Bureau	☐	☐
• The Social Welfare Insurance Center	☐	☐
• The Statistics Bureau	☐	☐
• The State Tax Bureau	☐	☐
• The Local Tax Bureau	☐	☐
• A bank (to document minimum capital requirements)	☐	☐
• The police (to register company seals)	☐	☐
• The local Career Service Center (to authorize recruiting employees)	☐	☐
• Trademark, Patent, and Copyright offices, as appropriate	☐	☐

Devising an entry strategy

Doing business in or with China can potentially provide many benefits, but not all entry modes provide every benefit. Knowing what areas are particularly important to your firm will help you determine the appropriate mode of entry and allow you to develop an entry strategy.

*Five-forces strategy—an entry strategy that evaluates: existing competitors; threat of new entrants; bargaining power of customers; bargaining power of suppliers; emergence of substitute products.

Defining your goals

Your first requirement is information. Conduct market research, use five-forces strategy* and obtain in-depth analysis of regulatory and legal details. Make a "business ecosystem" contact list of the major players—suppliers, investors, officials—that will influence your success in China. Once armed with this, you can start to formulate your business model.

BENEFITS OF DIFFERENT ENTRY MODES

POSSIBLE BENEFITS OBTAINED:	IMPORT FROM CHINA (BROKER)	EXPORT TO CHINA (BROKER)	JOINT VENTURE WITH CHINESE	WHOLLY FOREIGN-OWNED SUBSIDIARY
Low-cost supplier	Yes	No	Yes	Yes
Access to huge and growing market	No	Yes	Yes	Yes
Enjoy China's higher margins	No	Perhaps	Yes	Yes
Tap into China's talent pool	No	No	Perhaps	Yes
Strategic position vs. competitors	No	No	Perhaps	Yes
Business-friendly environment	No	No	Yes	Yes

PREPARE AN EXIT STRATEGY

It may seem fatalistic at this stage to consider a future retreat from your Chinese business venture, but it is vital that you pay early attention to exit strategies. Under both favorable and unfavorable conditions, how might your firm wrap up or liquidate its China investment?

Constructing a business model

Firstly, define your team. What core capabilities can your firm use to create a competitive advantage? What will your business partner ecosystem look like? Then, define the benefit or value you will create, both for your customers and for your firm.

Define your initial target customers. What specific group will highly value your firm's offering? What marketing and distribution channels will be the most effective in reaching this target customer?

Finally, define your financial model. What revenue stream will be created to make the new venture pay? What fixed and variable expenses will be incurred as you implement your business model? What is the expected life-cycle for these investments?

Fine-tuning your plan

By now your plan is beginning to take shape, but several important details need to be finalized:
• **Entry mode and sequence:** export/import, contract manufacturing, representative office, joint venture, or wholly foreign-owned subsidiary.
• **Entry location(s):** Bridge culture (such as Hong Kong), major urban areas, secondary cities, smaller cities, and rural communities.
• **Entry product(s):** Existing product/service, or extensively localized; product platform; brands, "whole solution."
• **Entry speed and ramp-up speed:** deterministic or event-based; incremental or seizing first-mover advantage.
• **Budget and financing:** cash flow, capital sources and cost, break-even point, rates of return.
• **Dealing with contingencies:** what elements and assumptions are important to your plan? How could these surprise you? How should your firm react?

Importing and exporting

Exporting to or importing from China requires proficiency with China's unique export logistics in addition to practical skills in import and export procedures. In-depth knowledge of restrictions, taxes, social concerns, financial arrangements, and professional resources will greatly aid your China export/import venture.

TIP

START SMALL
Test your import/export business plan with a modest-sized shipment, keeping a journal of problems, solutions, and resources that you uncover.

Understanding restrictions

China prohibits the export of certain items: media content related to national security (and this is very broadly defined); pre-1949 antiques; firearms and explosives; obscene material; toxic or hazardous materials; prisoner-made products; platinum; live plants, seed, and animals; and a variety of biological products. Prohibited imports include pornography; weapons; and toxic materials, but also e-waste (used computers, TVs, etc.); metallic scrap; industrial waste; and, again, certain published or electronic media content. In addition, the following imports may be restricted: goods that are subject to Chinese quotas, such as agricultural products and textiles; goods subject to Chinese import licensing, such as aircraft, cars, steel, and medicines; and strategically important goods, especially high-technology goods and those with potential military uses. Some nations license or prohibit this type of export to China, and products that can seem entirely innocent may be included in this category.

IN FOCUS...
ISO STANDARDS

The International Organization for Standardization (ISO) publishes 13,000 industry standards, some of which your firm may be required to meet. For example, ISO 9000 is the series of standards intended to document your firm's quality assurance procedures, and involves an in-depth investigation of your firm. ISO 9000 certification will greatly assist your firm in marketing its products in China, and will also help with marketing them in your home country.

Importing goods

Whether you import Chinese goods through a broker, have a long-term contract manufacture relationship, or actually employ Chinese workers in a Chinese subsidiary, it is vitally important that your firm understands and constantly monitors its value chain in order to maintain quality and, if appropriate, brand authenticity. Suppliers may sometimes substitute ineffective and even dangerous ingredients or components, or they may attempt to pass off counterfeit branded merchandise as authentic. Some may even falsely certify that they have met government-mandated safety and labelling requirements. Remember that once your firm's name goes on the package, it is you that becomes responsible for any intentional or unintentional errors or omissions, not only before the courts of law, but also in the court of public opinion.

Managing publicity

In a similar way, your product or service can receive very negative—and very costly—publicity if your Chinese suppliers or your Chinese managers fail to observe social policies that are of importance in your home country. Practices that may be legal, widespread, or even required in China can cause resentment, anger, and loss of reputation if reported in the media of your home country.

Labor conditions, worker safety, environmental protection, and government actions in China are a few of the areas that are frequently subject to miscommunication or distortion. Monitor your own operations and those of business partners for possible problem areas and resolve them in advance.

Warning signs to watch for when selling a product into China:

- Excessive demands for samples or prototypes

- Billing for travel, banquets, or gifts before negotiations

- Suggestions of shipments before payment is fully secured

- A buyer with little knowledge about the product

- Interest in your product or service that is unsolicited

- Destination addresses or shipping routes that seem unusual

- Promises to "bypass" any Chinese or WTO requirements

Inbound customs

Your freight forwarder or customs broker will handle the paperwork, inspections and fees related to import customs on your behalf. Be aware of those types of import that often require special procedures, such as food, cosmetics and medicines, clothing, furniture, and technology products. Depending on the nature, source, and destination of the goods, significant tariffs and fees might apply to your import/export goods. Imports that "fall through the cracks" and are not processed within a certain time limit are subject to sale by auction or to destruction, so learn your country's requirements ahead of time.

Freight forwarders

While it is your responsibility to understand the details of the export process, freight forwarders can provide vital services. Their role is to combine less than full container-sized shipments at origin, and disburse the various shipments on arrival. Experts in schedules and traffic management, they deal directly with sea, air, and overland carriers, and offer tracking and communications regarding the shipment. They undertake the formalities of shipping, including customs clearance, export and import tax payments, shipping fee payments, trade documentation, insurance and so forth.

Selling services

Advanced services are a major component of world GDP, and the import and export of services between China and other countries is proving to be an excellent opportunity for those prepared to conduct detailed background research and competition analysis. However, delivering a product can be relatively straightforward compared to the import and export of services or product/service packages. Services usually require some form of direct communication between the provider and client, with some types being more suited to certain market sectors. They include:

• A client visit to the provider—common in medicine, education, professional services, and tourism.
• A provider visit to the client—common in consulting, and in operations-related services.
• Remote delivery—common in out-sourced customer services, internet collaboration, teleconferencing, and e-business services.
• Provider establishes a service location abroad—used by most multinational corporations.
• Mixed delivery—for example, where part of the team interfaces with the client in person while research, design, or back-office support is provided abroad.

HOW TO... FIND A TRUSTWORTHY SHIPPING PARTNER

Seek business referrals through sources you trust (using your guanxi network)

↓

Get multiple credible references and verify them

↓

Accept only secure types of payment such as wire transfer or letter of credit

↓

Ask for a copy of the company's Chinese import/export license

↓

Contact your country's embassy in China and ask about any complaints

↓

Request a copy of the partner's Chinese business license and physically verify the address and other information

↓

Only deal with firms that have at least a few years of international trade experience

↓

If possible, obtain the sponsorship, support, or participation of influential Chinese individuals

Managing risk

Whether you plan on adding a single Chinese supplier or customer, or you need to create an entire business ecosystem in China, it is important to know your business associates. Knowing your associates in depth, and developing methods of obtaining real-time information about your associates' performance, are essential to your success in China.

*Due diligence—
the level of research
and investigation
that a reasonable
person would
normally conduct in
order to avoid harm.

STAY ON GUARD

Employee corruption is a problem in China. Supervise operations personally, and develop several Chinese-language sources for daily information about your business. Never have just one person handling orders, shipping payments, bank deposits, and accounting reconciliations.

Choosing new associates

Any seasoned China businessperson has heard stories of waste, fraud, and theft due to not knowing one's business associates. There is a distinct advantage in using both Chinese guanxi and Western due diligence* to select reputable and reliable partners.

• Interview your prospective business partner somewhere convenient for you, such as your hotel's restaurant. Taking a taxi across Shenzhen or Beijing can turn a 15-minute interview into an all-day project, especially if you add in an evening of karaoke.

• If you need a translator, bring your own. Ask probing questions that go beyond superficial aspects of your business, into the detail of the type of transactions you will employ. Ask questions relating to integrity.

• Get as many references as you can and, after the interview, carefully check all of them. Are they real? And from respected international firms? If they are the least bit suspicious, get a new set. If they have few or no credible references, you have your answer.

• For key business relationships, hire a professional investigator to verify the nature, capabilities, and financial stability of your prospective partner. Your embassy will be able to provide a list of reputable investigators; retired Hong Kong policemen make a speciality of this, and there is an investigative arm of the State Council in Beijing that has been known to accept private work.

Will your Chinese partners deliver?

There are three main levels of detail that require verification:

CONCEPTUAL LEVEL

- What level of quality do they see as "good enough"?
- How strictly do they observe a timetable or deadline?
- How much active management do they require?
- Are they proactive communicators?
- Can they provide active guidance or simply follow orders?

INDIVIDUAL AND COMPANY LEVEL

- Do they have recent experience in exactly this type of transaction?
- Did they do the work themselves or did an associate do it?
- Can they describe industry trends and key players in depth?
- Who ultimately owns the firm, and what are their goals?
- Can they provide multiple, credible references?

LEVEL OF CIRCUMSTANCES

- Does their company really exist? Does it exist as portrayed?
- Do they just want you for management or language training?
- Are they using you as a resource in securing other business?
- Do they just want to uncover and copy your business model?
- Is their main aim to direct your budget to friends and family?

Negotiating successfully with Chinese businesspeople

Negotiating in China is as much an art form as singing Beijing Opera or designing a courtyard garden. Your negotiating skills will be tested again and again, and attention to perfecting the details of your negotiating technique can bring you respect and fortune.

Understanding communications

BRIDGE THE GAP
Western people tend to conditionally trust strangers until there is some indication of bad intent. In China, strangers are viewed with suspicion and mistrust. Your negotiations are much more likely to succeed if attended by an intermediary who is trusted by both sides.

Negotiating any project requires highly proficient translation services; a major project may require primary and confirming translators. Regardless of the quality of the translation, you may find that most jokes, any subtle or eloquent speech, and very emotional or dramatic presentations do not translate at all well. Remember that in China "yes" usually means "I understand"; "no" (spoken by them or by you) may mean that negotiations have completely failed; and "we will consider your ideas" can mean either "no" or "we have to ask the boss," depending on who says it.

IN FOCUS...
THE BARGAINING GAME

Bargaining is a sport in China, and a rather arduous sport at that. Initial positions are usually very heavily padded to allow extended negotiations that may resemble a chess game without perceptible rules, and China's CEOs are the grand masters. Negotiating Chinese-style takes time. Often the first few meetings will seem like little more than social engagements, as participants share information about families, home towns, and leisure activities. But these meetings are not inconsequential—they begin the process of forming connections so essential to Chinese business. The rule is "friends first, business later."

TIP

**BUY YOURSELF
SOME TIME**
Refer to a higher
authority at the
beginning of the
negotiations—even
if they are fictitious—
who must be
consulted before
final approval. This
provides a face-
saving method for
exiting unsatisfactory
negotiations, without
permanently shutting
the door to a deal.

Meeting the right people

Your guanxi network should target an introduction
with top decision-makers, because in China,
meeting with lower-level staff is not very productive
and is an indirect way of saying "no thanks." A
meeting with a second-level manager can have the
opposite meaning, and might provide an opportunity
to explore bottom-line positions and "pre-negotiate"
delicate issues in order to reduce the risk of failed
negotiations at the higher level.

Starting with the easy issues

Don't over-strain any new relationship by tackling the
most difficult issues at the outset. Start by presenting
your strongest argument for reaching agreement on
the least controversial issue. Your secondary reasons
supporting an agreement should follow, until all your
evidence is presented. Once you have agreement on
that first "gateway" issue, you can forge ahead with
more controversial points.

Firming up the project

Expect successfully negotiated projects to begin
tentatively, with a memorandum of agreement or a
nominal transaction, and to accelerate as experience
and trust is gained. But once agreement has been
reached, even on very large projects, the Chinese
side will often act with surprising swiftness,
assembling materials, equipment, financing,
personnel, government approvals, and everything
else that is needed to make the project happen
immediately. Successful—and even sometimes less
than successful—negotiations are normally followed
by a long night of dining and socializing.

Resolving disputes with a Chinese business

Businesspeople test the borders of their agreements and perhaps Chinese business people test more aggressively than most. This makes some disputes a normal part of business in China, although for such disputes to go all the way to the courts is rare compared to the West.

TIP

DON'T ROLL OVER

"Backbone" is a term used in China to refer to influential or powerful supporters of your business who can step in to ensure a favorable result for any negotiated settlement. Negotiating important disputes is the time to use your backbone, as passive capitulation can lead to a loss of "face."

Understanding the process

There are four main methods of resolving business disputes in China: negotiation, mediation, arbitration, and litigation. All four are effective, but negotiation has the best chance of flexibly accommodating the changing needs of both parties.

Avoiding conflict is a key ideal of much Chinese philosophy—as Sun Tzu says in his famous *Art of War*, "Brambles grow where a great army has been, bad years follow a great war." In 1988 China had over one million neighborhood mediation committees, ruling on everything from debt collection to noisy neighbors. Chinese firms spend just 0.1 percent of the amount US firms spend on legal costs, based on percentage of revenues. This is due in part to the efficiency of negotiation and arbitration in resolving disputes, and in part to the shortage of plaintiff's attorneys. The Chinese legal environment is balanced and very welcoming for business, but, as elsewhere in the world, it is important to know and follow the law and deal with problems as early as possible.

Of course, the best method of resolving disputes is to avoid them: first, by dealing with business people you know very well and trust; secondly, by looking ahead to maintain your leverage in every foreseeable contingency; and thirdly, by knowing the details of your associates' actions.

Stages in dispute resolution

NEGOTIATION
Typical Chinese contracts require disputes to be negotiated within a certain time period before pursuing more forceful methods of resolution. In traditional Chinese business, an agreement is just a snapshot of the conditions that exist at the start of a relationship. Parties are expected to flexibly adjust their positions in response to changes in the business environment, rather than forcing one party to endure hardship.

MEDIATION
Historically, mediation has been the main tool for solving problems in China. Many businesses, including foreign-funded enterprises, have an internal mediation committee to solve minor disputes. The China International Economic and Trade Arbitration Commission (CIETAC) uses a blended mediation–arbitration format where, if the parties agree, an attempt at mediation is made before arbitration begins.

ARBITRATION
Ensure every contract you enter into provides for binding arbitration, if negotiation and mediation fail. It may specify one of the two Chinese arbitration bodies: CIETAC for general business disputes, and CMAC for those related to shipping—or a recognized international arbitration body. In China, arbitration is normally final, while court cases, even if won, can be appealed for years.

LITIGATION
Avoid litigation if at all possible. Remember that China's body of laws, precedents, and legal institutions are still evolving, and some courts are said to be overly swayed by policy or by local interests. If you do take a dispute to court, include both experienced Chinese lawyers and lawyers from international law firms on your legal team.

Index

Acknowledgments

Author's acknowledgments

I would like to thank the many participants in my teaching and training programmes at UC Berkeley, in Silicon Valley, and globally, for their valuable insights and questions about doing business in China.

I would also like to thank my many corporate and official supporters, in the US, China, and around the world for their generous contributions toward my research, which formed the foundation of this book. Their challenging problems and their demand for excellence has contributed greatly to my hands-on, real world knowledge of doing business in China.

Especially, I would like to thank my colleagues Professor AnnaLee Saxenian and Professor David Teece, long term friends and supporters of my work at the Center for Research on Chinese & American Strategic Cooperation at UC Berkeley.

Publisher's acknowledgments

The publisher would like to thank Professor Naresh Pandit, Tom Albrighton, Neil Mason, Sarah Tomley, Hilary Bird for indexing, and Chuck Wills for coordinating Americanization.

Picture credits

The publisher would like to thank the following for their kind permission to reproduce their photographs:

1 Alamy Images: Michael Kemp; 3 iStockphoto.com: blackred; 4–5 Corbis: Tibor Bognár; 8–9 iStockphoto.com: Frank van den Bergh; 13 iStockphoto.com: Julie Johnson; 18 Alamy Images: Ulana Switucha; 19 Alamy Images: Andrew Linscott; 21 Alamy Images: JLImages; 22–3 iStockphoto.com: magicinfoto; 26 iStockphoto.com: Scott Karcich; 31 Alamy Images: Joe Tree; 33 Alamy Images: K-PHOTOS; 38 Getty Images: Sigthor Markusson; 41 iStockphoto.com: auilovephoto; 45 iStockphoto.com: Andrew Cribb; 50–1 iStockphoto.com: Stefanie Timmermann; 52–3 iStockphoto.com: Hans Slegers; 55 Getty Images: Yukmin; 61 iStockphoto.com: Dragan Trifunovic; 62 Alamy Images: f1 online; 64 iStockphoto.com: Kristian Stensoenes; 64–5 cobalt id.

Every effort has been made to trace the copyright holders. The publisher apologizes for any unintentional omission and would be pleased, in such cases, to place an acknowledgment in future editions of this book.